Before You Publish

A Wellness Check-up With
Book Doctor, Robyn Conley

© 2014
Robyn Conley

Dedication/Acknowledgment

To my clients—my grandbabies in the making—for trusting me with their baby manuscripts and for pestering me to write this one!

Thank you and happy writing.

A Few Words About The Author

"Robyn Conley is one of those rare talents who in-
stinctively knows how to improve a sentence, paragraph or chapter. She also knows the contemporary
marketplace--who's buying what, what options authors
have, and what trends are affecting the publishing
industry. I have no hesitation in recommending
Robyn as a workshop presenter. She's always willing
to share her insights with others. Take advantage of
it. You won't regret it."

**--Ray Newton, Director of Reader's Digest Writing
Workshops, author of numerous articles and retired
instructor from Northern Arizona University**

"Robyn Conley always receives top ratings on evalu-
ations from participants who attend her workshops
and presentations. The Austin Writer's League is

fortunate to have access to her special talents and skills. Her most recent workshop was considered one of the best of the conference. When a writing group or workshop planner is looking for an expert on the topic of manuscript evaluation, the Austin Writer's League never hesitates to recommend Robyn."

--Angela Smith, former Executive Director, Austin Writer's League

"Everyone in the San Angelo Writer's club was well pleased. First and foremost, she focused on getting the writer published. Anyone who follows her recommendations WILL wind up with a professional manuscript that at least stands a chance of selling."

--Ken Hodgson, past President of the San Angelo Writer's Club

"We've had manuscript reviewers at our conferences before with mediocre results. This attitude abruptly changed with Robyn's appearance. She proved very knowledgeable and helpful in her reviews. Her methods were sound and productive. Probably her best attribute and most important for our conference: she seemed to care both about the manuscript and the person who wrote it. Participants felt like they had hours worth of information and insight into their writing abilities."

**--Will Miller, 1996 President of the Houston Manu-
scriptor's Guild**

"Based on Robyn's excellent and thorough critiques,
I sold my contemporary romance myself and later
found literary representation by submitting my
mainstream novel."

**--Dar Tomlinson, Scottsdale, AZ, Hemingway
Award Winner and author of numerous published
books including *Broken*, *A Risk of Rain*, and
*Designing Passion***

"Robyn Conley is the best bargain an aspiring writer
can get. She's informed, she's thorough--merciless,
actually--and she guides the writer through the rough
waters of early training so the creative process can
take over and pay off."

**--Gwen Choate, Nacodoches, TX, career author of
western novels, romance novels, and advertising
copy**

"Robyn's self-confidence and honesty made me trust
her. I rewrote the story and it won first place at
Southwest Writers Workshop conference. Now a
top book editor, top agent, and a top movie director
have my manuscript under consideration."

--Grace Cooley, Knoxville, TN, author of
Lost in Silence and Forgot

"I certainly appreciate all the help Robyn gave me. I felt I had an in-depth course in . . . well, just about everything about writing. I'm itching to start another project!"

--E.J. Phillips, Santa Fe, NM, author of *Woman: What She Has Done With Where She Has Been*

"Doc Conley helped me cure my novel's numerous grammatical blunders and noticed my characters suffered from a common speech impediment. She showed me a simple technique to give their dialogue movement, unique voice, and believable brevity. Robyn has the ear of a poet, the eye of an English professor, and the sensitivity of a children's author."

--Ron Jones, Carlsbad, NM, author of *The Dwarf and the Demon Tongue* and *Black Breath of the Lutron*

"Robyn excels in the field of Book Doctoring. Her recommendations for making your manuscript saleable are precise and to the point. Not only is she knowledgeable, but she is most encouraging. You get the feeling your work is as important to her as it is to you."

"Without the book doctor, *A Mouth Full of Shell* would not exist. She took the first draft and helped me find the rough patches that would turn a publisher off. But in that process she never, never disturbed my characters or plot. By putting her critiques in the form of questions that begin with 'can you,' 'might you,' or 'is it possible to', Ms. Conley held up a mirror to my pages so I could see them more clearly. Because of these qualities, she was a joy to work with, and an editor to cherish."

--Connie Gotsch, Farmington, NM, author of *A Mouth Full of Shell*

Table Of Contents

What to Know Before You Publish

Introduction

After typing the final word of their books, articles, or short stories many writers E-mail me to ask, "What's next?" Most of them think my immediate response will be, "Publish!" Some often pump my brain for agent or editor names.

I understand. After all, I'm a writer first, so my heart knows the need we writers have to see our work in print.

For this reason I've listed the various types of publishing options first in this book and then followed up with detailed revision tips. Our work will most likely only be published after we take time to revise, but we can't help ourselves. We have to dream of the big publishing picture first!

So, without guilt, study the various publishing options, from the large traditional publishers to the smaller, independent publishers, to those who only offer E-books. Today we're blessed with more choices than ever in the history of writing.

Keep in mind, however, revision is always a crucial next step before submitting to any of those publishers. As revisionists with our writing, we must be as objective as possible in the process. Achieving that objectivity takes a certain amount of study along with a certain amount of practice.

This book will give you the tools you need to evaluate your work with new eyes. It is an interactive guide, providing detailed discussion and instruction, examples and exercises that will show you how to become your own book doctor. It will also show you how to research a variety of avenues regarding publication of your projects.

You'll learn answers to questions such as:

**Is there sufficient character conflict and resolution, or setting and sensory details that enhance mood?

Content and flow questions are addressed.

**What is POV, and is first person POV really the best choice for this particular novel?

Structure and theme issues are discussed.

**Have you chosen an informative approach to "Traveling with Rover," when it could be stronger, i.e. more marketable, such as a how-to?
   The importance of format to enhance specific topics is stressed.

   You'll also find basic revision examples involving dialogue necessities, punctuation, repetitive words and prepositional phrases, etc., along with the key problems embedded in most submission packages.

   Finally if you've examined, treated and bandaged all the sentences you can, yet still feel your work needs a second opinion, you'll find advice about how to secure a qualified, honest, and dependable book doctor or freelance editor to help you make your prose healthy and ready to send out into the marketplace.

Publishing Basics

So what are you marketing? Poetry? How-to articles? Novels? Sometimes we writers have several types of writing to offer at one time. With a little homework, we can find niche markets for just about anything we create. And as long as you don't mind taking the time to study, you will find outlets for your words.

The most basic of the basics is research. Let's say you want to find a home for a vignette you wrote about your military days. Perhaps the main focus was leadership, or friendship, or overcoming fear or harsh elements. Do you see where I'm going with this? No matter the actual paragraph by paragraph construction of your vignette, there are already a few ideas for different types of markets.

One market might be military magazines or

veteran group newsletters. Another type would be any websites in a similar vein. Others might include a leadership organization or more of a generic lifestyle magazine, depending on the main focus of the vignette.

Homework. Finding publishers for your writing takes research—good old fashioned homework. I'm no longer surprised at how many writers E-mail me wanting me to find publishers for them, but I am dismayed. Even if I wanted to, I could never scrounge enough time to research all the markets for all the genres of all the word counts of all the publishers.

The most basic rule of submitting to publishers of any type is researching what they publish and how they prefer to receive their submissions. You can use books such as the *Writer's Digest Writer's Market*, which gives greater details in your hand about most major and small book publishers, as well as regional and independent presses. Writer's Digest also offers this information online if you subscribe to that service.

Another option is typing your topic into your browser's search bar, along with "publishers" beside it. Soon you'll have dozens of options to further research. Let's focus now on both the traditional and small presses.

Traditional Publishers

When you're researching major publishers, you'll soon discover many of the "biggies" will only accept manuscripts through agents. If you're hard set on submitting to only those publishers, you'll need to step back from researching publishers and now focus on researching agents.

It's the same process: type in your topic, followed by "agents" and begin browsing the internet for possible matches. One other way is to scan a wonderful book by Jeff Herman, titled, *Guide to Book Publishers, Editors, and Literary Agents*. He offers terrific insider information about each agent that you might not find in a generic listing on their websites.

Here's the harsh reality of focusing solely on major publishers or seeking agent representation: timeframe. Let's say you study the pubs, find one you crave as a publisher for your book, and choose an agent to send your manuscript to for possible representation.

Most agents will reply to your query somewhere within two months after receiving it. If they want to see more of your work, they'll ask for an exclusive read, meaning you should not submit it to any other agent or publisher, while they evaluate the entire manuscript. Even so, you can expect another two months or longer for a complete read and response.

Keep in mind 90% of writers are still rejected at this stage, including writers with other published credits in their bios.

At the least, four months have passed with zero progress toward publication. The hard truth is most of the traditional publishers buy from authors with large audiences, meaning well-established authors or self-help speakers with millions of followers or media personalities who offer books to cross-market their work.

Most of us ordinary writers don't fit into those categories. Fear not, we have other options!

Small Presses & Regionals

Some writers' prose is more regional in nature, meaning they write about travel in Missouri, or pen historical vignettes for their local paper. These shorter pieces might lead in the direction of a book length collection of articles, all connected with a fresh theme. Buyers for such an item would be small regional presses.

Other small presses focus on one type of literary writing, such as short fiction or themed poetry selections. Many anthologies of all genres are published by small presses.

Often a small press is a good starter publisher for a freelance author who is ready to branch out into a published book format. Some of the pluses of small presses are their willingness to work with lesser-known writers and their more open communication with writers. Some of the negatives include nominal or zero advances and a limited market.

At this point, it's imperative to realize no publisher, whether a larger traditional or a smaller/regional press, will help much with increasing your readership.

Creating your audience is all about your dedication to selling your books through your website and through your personal contact with people. Honest to goodness, that's the actuality of publishing your writing with ANY of these options, especially when choosing one of the next three categories.

Self-publishing
Print on Demand Technology
E-books

When choosing to self-publish, it's imperative to comprehend the definition of Print on Demand Technology (POD) as well as E-books.

First of all POD brings magical low cost printing to the masses of authors. It's the type of printing used by the CreateSpace folks, as well as countless other instant publishers now crowding the industry with their preferred book lists. Some of the most popular include: Xlibris, iUniverse, Infinity, and dozens upon dozens of others. We used to call these presses "vanity" publishers, and basically they are the same today, although much less expensive.

Writers pay these companies to set-up their books into printable format and print out one, or one hundred, or more copies. We can choose any number of options regarding layout, cover design, and level of proofing/copyediting.

Dangers lurk in these avenues for writers who have not compared the variety of companies, including the costs and the finished products. I can't even begin to list the books I've seen with typos on the covers and incorrect sentence structure within the text. These are some of the worst problems with self-publishing and the POD companies. They may promise a quality editing/proofing if a writer buys that "package option," however the reality is something horrifying.

On the flip-side, writers with a network of fellow writers who can help polish their works to a high, error-free shine, can then upload their writing with little worry.

Next, these writers must be realistic about MARKETING their books, whether they're fiction or non-fiction. They'll need to make sure their books are also available in E-book format, so any reader with a Nook or Kindle, or a tablet can easily download that book with a click of a button. This means self-publishing with a vanity press must include setting up a website with a page offering your books for sale in both print and in E-book options.

Here's the emphatic reminder: you'll need to be willing to sell your books via a website AND in-person regardless of whether a traditional publisher takes you on, or a small/regional press accepts you, or whether you choose to self-publish.

Now you have the big picture truths: you must be willing to sell as well as write, AND you must be willing to write well first. You do this by studying the craft, which is by far the most crucial step in becoming a quality writer. We'll examine those processes in greater detail throughout the rest of the book.

A Professional Diagnosis

SIGNING THE CONSENT FORM

How many afternoons have turned you into a swivel chair captive, rewriting a first paragraph? Page? Entire chapter? You search for the most descriptive metaphor, or weigh verb after verb, praying to choose the "correct" one.

Unfortunately, sometimes you're so desperate to write fresh phrases, you end up sabotaging your creativity. Not a healthy regimen. But how can you overcome any insecurity and move forward, allowing your pens and keyboards a free rein? Learning this crucial first step may be the most vital element in crafting both fiction and non-fiction.

Although most modern physicians believe in healing the whole body, even old Dr. Frankenstein started with little more than a skeleton. Like the infamous doctor, writers must add muscle and cosmetic details to their creations, molding them into a solid foundation most commonly referred to as the rough draft. And if this first draft is the skeleton, then the blank page is the consent form.

Henriette Klauser, Ph.D., owner of Writing Resources, and author of *Writing on Both Sides of the Brain*, as well as several other writing books, encourages her students to "rapid write." They're asked to choose a specific amount of time, and write non-stop (about anything), for the designated span. The exercise underscores the necessity of filtering those ricocheting thoughts onto paper before they're lost to our rambling minds.

A similar idea David Hughes terms the "10-Minute Timed Torrent" was drilled into his head during a creative writing workshop at UCLA. In just six months, David accumulated two short story wins, became the "Toaster" contributor in *Courier* magazine, and enjoyed numerous other publishing credits. He still uses this trick today.

Basically, both processes grant you permission to write garbage. It doesn't matter which plot pattern, character sketch, or great non-fiction idea you conjure first. The lesson is learning to let go with what you're writing. Let go of apprehension. Accept the fact that mistakes will be made, and realize every successful writer once worried over similar goofs. Believe you can write as well as anyone else scribbling down a rough draft. And, most importantly, don't allow guilt over comma splicing, too much passive voice, or a preponderance of pronouns render your imagination empty.

Even best-selling authors must struggle through a first draft. Janet Dailey, referred to as one of the five all-time best selling authors, never revises until she finishes a complete manuscript. At a recent workshop she shared one major tip she uses for staying in the writing chair each day until that writing deadline is met. "I work everyday and I only write five pages. Not more, not less, just five. Very seldom do I complete a sentence at the end of the fifth page. The next morning I reread that last sentence, pick up the creative flow again, and charge ahead until I finish my five pages."

There are many other tricks to letting go and writing. Dusty Richards, renowned western novelist and Spur award winner, is also a popular speaker at many writing conferences. He advises: "Link it to bike riding and the wobbly first time you set out on it without training wheels--you have to learn. Keep pedaling. Don't stop to figure out how the wheels are rolling."

When award-winning author Pat Haley has trouble moving forward with her rough drafts, she doesn't go back and edit; she reads novels in her genre. Reading helps her pick up the momentum and return to her own work. "Either that, or I'll mentally start lecturing, reminding myself I really am a grown-up and I can do this if I'll just relax." No doubt her combination of both strategies keeps her writing and winning.

Of course, there are those times when you're just plain stuck. Electrical engineer, Carl Krause, writes numerous business proposals and lengthy technical texts in his job. He says he begins each project with an outline, then if he hits a snag, he jumps ahead, "to the next place in the outline if I start dragging." The point is to keep that creative drive engaged, even if you have to switch gears.

Recently, a young visitor to our read and critique group listened wide-eyed as one of the more advanced writers read a chapter from her novel. After we adjourned, he confided, "I'll never be able to write that good." Maybe, maybe not. Certainly not if he never completes the rough draft.

So, as Dr. Klauser encourages, train your mind to function in the manner best suited to the project at hand. The right brain should be given freedom to trample along the least traveled roads of your subconscious, poking amongst the underbrush for plotting ideas and character traits. The best way to do that is to run stark naked with your creativity.

Don't be afraid to bare those virgin thoughts, no matter how your conscious mind chastises the behavior.

You might want to try one of the free-writing exercises mentioned, or others like the "mapping" technique explained in Barry Lane's book, *Writing as A Road to Self Discovery*. I usually call it "bubbling" when I use this exercise in my Reduce Stress workshops. It's a fun and insightful tool that helps people identify factors lying in their subconscious that might attribute to brain strain or negative emotions. For a writer, the process works like this:

1) On a blank piece of paper, jot down a major element of your story, whether a plot point, a character, or theme issue.

2) Circle it.

3) Now draw a line from that word and jot down whatever pops into your mind. Circle it.

4) Continue that process, as words tumble from your imagination into "bubbles" on the page.

When you've bubbled for a while, put down your pen and study your brainstorming session. Do you see any new plot possibilities or character traits emerging that you might have overlooked before? If it's a non-fiction piece, did you come up with new research directions or alternate angles of approaching your theme or topic?

Another solid source for keeping your creativity moving forward is Jack Heffron's *The Writer's Idea Book*. It is chock full of great jumping off exercises, such as:

PROMPT: Choose a character from a project you're working on or planning to begin. Ask him to explain his beliefs, even if only in a scattered, elliptical way. Try to dig into the character's mind and let him talk to you, without forcing it. Put the page away for a few days, then return to it. Any surprises? Does it make sense? Does it fit the character as you knew him? Here's another:

PROMPT: Write about a time when you did something hurtful, but did not feel guilty. Explore the emotional complexities of the situation and your reaction to it. Then write a scene in which a female character professes feelings of guilt, but clearly does not feel that way. Use action, gesture, and voice to signal her true feelings.

Each of these prompts involves taking an infant thought as a primary jumping off point, and then filtering through the natural emotional and imagery process that follows.

Many non-fiction writers use list-making as a free writing prompt to help organize thoughts and structure for articles and books. If you're writing an opinion or persuasive piece, you'll want to look at both sides of an issue and be able to qualify your thoughts with quotes from experts, facts and statistics. If you're writing a "how-to" project, listing the order of progression is essential before filling in secondary information.

After doing the preliminary writing, you should summon the left brain's editing capabilities--but not a moment sooner. This is the one occasion when my book doctor's persnickety persona actually promotes procrastination. Allowing the sedative of time to work for your manuscripts may be as important as getting the first words written--and it may be just as difficult.

GIVING ANESTHESIA ITS DUE

First, accept the fact that nobody's rough draft whizzes from the printer in Pulitzer condition, and then set the manuscript aside for a day, a week, or even longer if possible. For me, taking an editing time-out proves the hardest part. The emotional high you experience when holding those freshly inked pages is sometimes hard to resist. Whether you've written a whole chapter, a short story or 1000-word article, you naturally want to read and revise right away.

"You're rushing again, aren't you?" Thank goodness I have an editing buddy who isn't afraid to chide me into responsibility after I've handed her something without a proper down time. Rewriting too soon after creating not only hampers your objectivity, but that lack of objectivity endangers your sales potential.

No matter how aggravating it seems to wait, lay aside your latest literary masterpiece for as long as possible. You might consider working on another project. It worked for Rupert Hughes, a popular writer during the early 1900s. His short stories and novels appeared in the top magazines of his day, and were later published in book form. Sam Goldwyn was so impressed by Hughes' talent that he talked the author into traipsing across the country from New York to California to write for "moving pictures."

Rupert Hughes remained prolific in a day before word processors or even electric typewriters because he had several desks in his office. He even had one built at a height comfortable for him to work at while standing. If he tired of sitting, he could keep writing. Each sit-down desk had a different writing project on it, so when he felt blocked on one project, he moved to another.

WHAT ABOUT DEADLINES?

Right. Unfortunately, deadlines at this point can be cumbersome. What should you do when you're on a tight schedule--with no luxury of allowing those newborn words time for your editing sensibilities to adjust? You might try one of these practical ideas that have helped me and other writers battle both tight schedules and the over-anxious desire to edit:

1) **Take a walk**--not in some irresponsible huff, mind you--but rather a leisurely stroll to temper your left brain's editing urges. You'll be pleasantly surprised how even an hour's span, physically away from those tempting words, will broaden your viewpoint regarding content and style.

2) **Call in a second pair of eyes**--either fax, E-mail, or deliver a hard copy of your work to a trusted critic. Don't be embarrassed because you've dropped off a first draft. Another writer's objectivity can help you mold the piece for a faster turnaround, and beware--waiting to the last minute can test your sanity. One of my clients worked all afternoon trimming a ten-page synopsis to one page per requirements for a contest deadline the next day. By evening, she couldn't stomach another look at it, and she had certainly lost her objectivity. She called me, frantic, knowing she needed to at least proof it with fresh eyes, but she was out of time. Considering this happened before the days of E-mail and she didn't own a fax machine, I suggested she read her synopsis--with every mark of punctuation--while I typed it onto my screen. Thank goodness she'd already pared it to half its original length! Together

we reworked her material until she had a polished version to slip in the mail the next morning.

3)   Attack that mound of 'busy' work—a perfect opportunity to file those magazine and newspaper articles you've clipped and stuffed behind the Rolodex. Double-check your submission records. Do you have any manuscripts needing a follow-up letter to the editor? Maybe you're running low on enve-lopes, or ink cartridges. What better time to make a quick supply list? Whatever your option, the point remains--a little distance and a second opinion breed a whole lot of perspective. The trick is finding the most workable means for gaining insight, without diving into the editing waters unprepared.

A few years ago when my son was a wise 6th grader, he overheard me reading and re-reading a troublesome spot in a client's manuscript. I didn't know he'd been eavesdropping until he stuck his head around my door and said, "Uh…Mom, my teacher told us it's not polite to read out loud when we're old."

"Impolite," I corrected, without thinking first. Since I edit in a home office, I sometimes react involuntarily before snapping back into mother mode. Then my brain caught up to what he'd said. I chose to let the 'old' crack slide, annoying him instead by lecturing him about how reading out loud helps us hear our mistakes or problem areas. Of course, he rolled his eyes and abandoned my office.

In Natalie Goldberg's book, *Wild Mind, Living the Writer's Life*, she also reiterates the value of reading your work out loud: "It's part of the writing process, like bending down to touch your toes and then standing up again. Write, read, write, read. You become less attached to whether it is good or bad."

Actually, her exercise reference isn't such a stretch, considering the similarities between rewriting and athletic training. Each time you read your work aloud, you tone the manuscript's body toward optimum fitness. Just as a marathon runner cross trains, you must also build your literary pecs, shaping your work into taut, tingling prose.

Harlequin author, Linda George, once said, "Readers say the words in their minds, so, I know if I trip over a phrase while reading aloud, they will, too." She also thinks television's immediate visual references have led to a more auditory style of writing. "Many novels written today must be oriented toward possible movie deals or audio books. The words have to flow off the tongue so the narrating celebrity doesn't stumble or stutter. Try reading *Walden* aloud, then pick up a bestseller by Stephen King or Dean Koontz. You'll immediately notice a difference in pace, sentence length, word placement, and choice."

One writer said she watches others' expressions while reading her work to a critique group so she can ". . .see if what I wrote had the effect I wanted."

Patricia Wrede, a fellow writer, recently shared what she's noticed during critique sessions: "Reading work, particularly out loud, is an excellent way to spot certain kinds of errors in dialogue (like tongue twisters) that no real person could ever say without stumbling."

Yet, she also has a caution to add: "Reading in a critique group can lead to a poorer quality critique. A good reader can make bad writing sound good. A bad reader can make good writing boring. I've seen both happen. Furthermore, the author knows what every sentence is 'supposed' to say and reads it with appropriate emphasis. This effectively disguises sentences which are ambiguous or unclear."

Still, reading out loud helps us "hear" our written thoughts, even though some writers balk at the thought of reading in front of their peers. A compromise Patricia suggests, and one we often implemented in my group, is delegating someone other than the author to read the manuscript. This practice guarantees the benefits of a verbal run-through, without allowing any preconceived intonations to filter through from the reader. Also, having someone else read your work is a lifesaver for authors totally debilitated by the thought of reading out loud.

Good-natured Dusty Richards advocates both

reading in a critique group and reading in solitude. "Without a critique group, I feel sorry for you. I use mine to death and they tear me apart. Second best thing is to read aloud into a tape recorder--cheap one from Wal-Mart's just fine. Then play it back. When you read it out loud, you sometimes put in the right word that needs to be there, but might be missing from your page. Listen to it a second time. Your ear is a great perceiver of what is right, plus, the cross-check can make your corrections even stronger."

Regardless of which "auditory therapy" you choose, specific elements should be kept in mind during the read. Most of these essentials center around flow and content. During this phase, con-centrate on whether character thoughts and actions, or background and setting details, come together in ways that enhance the story line or angle. You want to listen for any stumbling blocks in sections of long narrative. Are there enough sensory and visual specifics to create a believable setting? Always try to include multiple senses to heighten the reader's immersion into the world you've presented. What is your character smelling, hearing, feeling on his or her skin? All this must be accomplished in a natural flow, without sounding like you've gone down a description check list, plugging in a weathered thicket of trees here, followed by a cloudless sky there, and a pastel colored mesa bringing up the rear.

One tricky area my clients run into is describing their characters. Can we see them clearly, or are we jerked into a blatant physical sketch featuring her green eyes, a nose longer than her hair, and feet wading in soupy toes? Also, remember to build the characters' actions and reactions in a logical style, maintaining their personalities and appropriate growth within the story's development. It really is best to let the reader get to know your characters the same way we get to know people: a little at a time.

Search for places to pique the reader's interest—maybe insert a startling fact, or questionable character motive. Some editors believe a reader's enthusiasm declines after the original, catchy hook. With that in mind, keep this checklist nearby when reading your latest creation out loud:

1)   Make sure you haven't lapsed into puzzling points of view. If you have more than one character's thoughts clogging any paragraph, separate those perspectives.

2)   Check your dialogue and tags to determine if the speakers and reactions are clear by your sentence structure.

3)   Remember to review tenses. Shifting from the past into the present isn't allowed in fiction—except during time travel novels, and even then, rarely in the tenses.

Before progressing to the next read-through, ponder Sheridan Baker's thoughts from his book, *The Complete Stylist*. "In writing (reading), you clarify your own thoughts. Indeed, you probably grasp them for the first time.... In the end, after you have rewritten and rearranged, your words will carry your readers to see as you see, to believe as you believe, to understand your subject as you now understand it."

Part III

Doctoring Fiction

Toning Literary Muscle

When I critique a novelist's work, I sometimes feel like an Olympic judge, offering red-penned marks for plot development, characterization, scene structure and emotional tension, not to mention dialogue and a story's believability factor. The wonderful difference between what I do and what the judges do is instead of offering a brusque set of points, I get personal.

I saturate the margins, sometimes with notes of praise when a bit of dialogue is especially biting or authentic, but most often I scribble constructive comments. Lots of them. Ask any of my clients and they'll attest to dripping pages of notations and suggestions. The more honest among them will also admit I have a doctor's poor penmanship, but the grandbabies on my "Published Clients" bookshelf prove that those writers who have deciphered my comments have also made their work better and their weaknesses non-existent. You can do that for your writing, too. It just takes practice.

Characterization

CARING--

One of my favorite workshops is titled, "GUTS: Making a Good Story Great." Like all my workshops, it's interactive, but this one allows the writers to really sink their teeth into their characters, so by the end of the session we've all had fun playing "make believe."

During one particular exercise, the writers toss out details about their characters they've rediscovered through a previous exercise, and man oh man—let me tell you there are some really imaginative storytellers out there!

The exercise is called, "Care-actor." First and foremost we, as readers, have to CARE about your main character. To care about that character, we have to believe that the person is real, with faults as well as interesting and admirable traits. This is an especially important task in a flash fiction or short story, when that character must snatch our emotions early. Accomplishing this takes some brain time. The way I stretch writers' imaginations in my workshop is to ask them to place their character in a vehicle.

The type of vehicle should reflect the character's personality. For instance, you wouldn't have a modern multi-million dollar businesswoman driving a beat up Dodge Ram into the triple level-parking garage. Or maybe you would if your intent was to show a quirky, non-traditional side to her character, or a temporary snag in her income situation, i.e. to set up a conflict. With that in mind, try this little exercise on for size. Take the main character from a novel or short story you're working on, and then put them behind a steering wheel:

> **Name the kind of vehicle.**

> **List three things about the interior upholstery/exterior paint.**

> **List three things the character sees when adjusting the rear-view mirror.**

> **Show us the type of clothes that should be secured under the seatbelt.**

> **Pick out a snack or drink that the person dribbles onto his or her chest.**

> **List three items found on the passenger seat.**

> **List three things placed inside the glove box.**

> **List three things stashed in the trunk.**

Now, study the verbs I used in the last three statements. Those verbs imply that there might be items in those locations not first thought of when the reader originally envisions your character. That's good! It's the best way to set up the believability factor for those surprises that must be laced throughout your writing. Creating a solid character foundation is crucial to the fresh feel of your story, and it often means the difference between a sale or rejection.

GROWTH / PLOT PROGRESSION--

Caring isn't enough for a sale, however; we must also worry about your character. And we'll want that worry justified at the story's end! Just as every character must face a conflict in the opening of the story, each conflict must build before being resolved. And it darn sure better be resolved. Many beginning writers have seen my red pen explode on the final page of their work if they've left me hanging without wrapping up the details of the character's motivation.

It is crucial for a writer to remember that the initial conflict needs to have a believable reference and closure by the story's end. Notice I did not say a rosy, happily ever after closure. Any authentic tidying up will do, but it must be there in a blatant overtone, whether through dialogue or narrative. We must know that the inner motivation that spurred the character early on has had a progression and finalization.

What inner motivation you say? Let's take a peek at what Tom Sawyer, head writer and producer of the hit, *Murder She Wrote* has to say about building characters and their motivations in his new book, *Fiction Writing Demystified*:

"Most of us learn early on to begin developing our characters by writing brief bios, three, four lines, more as we learn more about them.... But what's really important to your story...are: what are the lines of conflict between this character and the other characters? Where's the heat? Where are the problems? The pain? The one-sided abrasiveness? What does each want—and is having a hard time getting? How do their goals clash with the interest of the other players? Are two or more of them pursuing the same ends? Will the achievement of one character's goal—the journey that gets him there—cost the well-being or life of another character? Will it cost him his own soul?"

What Tom knows is that television viewers, as well as fiction readers, expect the character they've cared and worried about from the beginning to grow and learn, maybe even change a little from the way they first saw that character. And they want the character to digest those revelations as he or she encounters the plot circumstances that bring about any shifts in their thoughts or behavior.

Maybe you have a selfish jock suddenly thrust into a situation where he has to weigh the advantages or disadvantages of helping someone rather than himself. How will that affect the team he's leading? Is the final score the only answer? Better yet, make that character a female to break tradition.

Tension thrives when the conflict, either inner or outer, builds a little with each scene. Fiction lives or dies by the scene choices a writer makes, and those choices are still based in character. What's at stake for the character in this scene? How will the character's thoughts, emotions, or behavior be affected by what happens next?

Each scene is a stepping-stone in plot, yes, but also in character development. Some novice writers reverse the process and think plot is more important than character. Not so.

Best selling author, Anne Lamott, says: "Plot grows out of character.... Characters should not, conversely, serve as pawns for some plot you've dreamed up. Any plot you impose on your characters will be onomatopoetic: PLOT. I say don't worry about plot. Worry about characters. Let what they say or do reveal who they are, and be involved in their lives, and keep asking yourself, Now what happens?"

Such great insight, but my favorite bit of advice from Ms. Lamott is: "Find out what each character cares about most in the world because then you will have discovered what's at stake."

Or, "Where's the heat?" as Tom Sawyer asked.

When you can do that chapter-by-chapter, that's when you've learned out how to keep the tension mounting throughout an entire novel, paragraph-by-paragraph for a short story, and line-by-line in flash fiction.

One major advantage of incorporating this care factor and conflict factor into each scene, is you automatically avoid holes in your writing. If someone has ever read your current story and said they had trouble connecting with the character or following the plot, then examine each scene for a lack of character motivation. I bet you'll be able to fill in those voids with ease.

Genre Breakdowns/Responsibilities

Of course as soon as we learn about character and plot necessities, we also must beware of genre-sensitive elements. For example, in romances—in all the various categories—you must have the male and female meet in chapter one and the conflict that keeps them apart needs to show up right away, too.

In cozy mysteries, there better be a dead body in the opening scene or you've eliminated yourself as a mystery writer. And if you use a detective or P.I. in first person, you'll have to be extra careful not to overuse the "I" sentence starters. More about that in Part V.

Thrillers, sometimes called suspense, MUST have a "world risk consequence" factor and they must be fast-paced. I had one client who told me he enjoyed writing his long sentence structure because it gave his readers something to chew on like a fine piece of prime rib. Well, maybe so, but leave those sentences to a different genre than thriller/suspense. These types of books need a fresh voice, a good mix of quick sentences when the action is mounting and a lot of dialogue that keeps the pace and plot pumping.

Science fiction and Fantasy writers sometimes mistakenly think they can toss in an element of technology or magic in the middle of the book, or worse, in the final climax, without first setting up a believability factor for it early on in the novel. Many of my clients have done this in their first writing endeavors and have had to restructure from the beginning. No problem if you want your cat-like character to use its extendable, 12-inch claws to win the final battle, BUT if up to that point in the story, we think the character's only unique feature is its extra-long, sharp fingers, well, then you've cheated the reader.

After saying that, I don't mean you have to blatantly list the elements that mold your characters and your setting. Use your creativity to imply that something unusual might be under the surface, so to speak. Maybe someone the cat-like character comes into contact with mentions her lovely long fingers, and she says something like, "Thank you, they've come in quite handy when I'm in a bind." See how that reference implies, but doesn't give all away? So, as long as you make sure you set up your "other world" and its characters in a believable manner, then you'll do fine.

Westerns certainly don't have to be set in the old west these days. There are a lot of contemporary types being written around Pro rodeo and other concerns of a modern cowboy and rancher. But the good guy/bad guy elements must be strong; there must be action right away; and there better be some authentic dialogue that represents solid characterization, not stereotypical cardboard figures.

And then there's a cloudy mix of mainstream, contemporary women's and literary fiction that isn't really a genre in so many words, but more of an ominous category where the rules of genre writing are smashed to smithereens. Yet these books have somehow stolen an editor's interest and found publication. Everyone wants to succeed in this category. Few do. There are other types of novels that fit absolutely nowhere in any genre or category.

Bottom line: if you're writing in a certain genre, then study the requirements of that genre. Then go the next step further and study each publisher's preferences for that genre. You'll be surprised to learn that many editors at various publishing houses prefer no flashbacks, no first person, no prologues, etc. These details can appear endless. They can detract from the reason you picked up the pen in the first place. But, when you do your homework as well as write from the heart with quality craft and passion, you WILL succeed in setting your voice out there for all to read.

Voice and Style Issues

I have a book on my shelf titled, *Writer's Inc* (D.C. Heath and Company). Simple, concise, and well organized, the book is really a high school grammar book and one I wished I had back in the dark ages of sophomore English class. Regarding voice it offers these insights:

Samuel Johnson, a noted writer of the eighteenth century, was undoubtedly talking about one of the greatest temptations facing writers—to use lots of big words (big words, clever words, fancy words). For some reason, we get into our heads the idea that writing simply, is not writing effectively. Nothing could be further from the truth.

The very best writing is ordinary and natural, not fancy or artificial. ... It is your best chance at a personal style. A personal voice will produce natural, honest passages you will not have to strike out.

As I've often shared in workshops, voice and style go hand in hand. All writers wouldn't agree with me. No doubt certain college English profes-sors would enjoy discussing the differing nuances for days. But as the quote above emphasizes, your natural voice is what enhances your writing style. Finding that voice often determines your life and breath as a writer. Perhaps you've decided that voice and style are ambiguous--vague elements that you'll never master.

Please.

Sure, you have to practice, practice, practice until that jumble of words emanating from the pages represents your authentic voice and style, but you can do it, often easier than you first believed.

How do you do it? Think about this: if you spoke your story out loud, what type of words would you choose? What type of sentences would work best for you? Short? Long? Medium? Actually a good mix of sentence structure is the best, but finding the mix that suits you is the key.

Some of my clients have told me they use a recorder early on in their writing to help them "hear" the voice and style. Doing this, they learn what is most similar to their spoken word choices and the arrangement of those words. This is helpful to a degree, IF you remember that your reader needs to be able to follow at a comfortable pace.

For example, in my everyday conversation, I'm a mumbler, speaking in joined phrases that zip through my noggin with little organization. Often my first drafts appear in that style. And although the voice is accurate, I have to go back and clean up those meandering phrases--smoothing some places into cleaner sentences until a more varied structure and presentation emerges. By the time I've finished revising and tweaking, the end product represents what has become my best writing style.

Jill Millican, a successful commercial scriptwriter, has a different voice and style for her memoir writing than the one she uses for her professional scriptwriting. When reading her memoir manuscript filled with stories about the years she taught in-- what is referred to in politically correct terms as--an economically disadvantaged school district, I heard a compassionate, knowledgeable, sometimes tired voice. Every so often, however, there was a haunting edge of reality.

Usually these passages announced a harsh visual: a rumpled, hungry first grader who had to dress himself for school and skipped breakfast because his mother was a passed out crack addict; or a child sick with a fever who Jill fashioned a pallet for behind her teacher's desk because the mother worked nights at a local strip joint and took the phone off the hook to sleep during the day.

When I asked Jill if she would mind sharing a bit of her memoir manuscript in this book to help illustrate my comments about voice and style, she also generously offered these words regarding voice:

Finding your voice in reflective writing is like discovering, relatively late in life, that you have always been in love with the boy next door. Your voice, like your past, is the sum total of your experiences. The words you use are a vehicle that allows you to take someone on that journey with you.

Maybe it's not something I let everyone see on a daily basis, but I'm never far from the breathless ten-year old who played flashlight tag at twilight with the kids down the block, or the restless preadolescent who built a fort with her first boyfriend in a crabapple tree. Moments that we compare experiences to are like the slow de-termined inner voice, imposing order and mean-ing to otherwise unnoticed ideas, which becomes our writing. Our voice is nothing if it is not sim-ply--us.

Finding my own voice for the first time was an identity crisis. I even went so far as to send Robyn a copy of a novel I read which had a style that intrigued me. Would this work for me? Is this a way to structure the non-fiction manuscript I'd been working on? A patient mentor, Robyn kept encouraging me to be myself. There are no other viable options.

If your first love is your truest love, then the voice you write with is the voice you've had all along. It's the voice you used to scribble out hurried essays in school, the voice that muses in your journal, the voice that writes a chatty letter to your best friend. It is the boy next door.

And here is a brief portion from her memoir. While reading it, compare any similarities and any differences from her style and voice in the above segment to the excerpt:

Prologue

My job interview was deceptively familiar. At first glance, Shady Grove looked like the kind of elementary school I attended as a child...an older brick building surrounded by post-World War II matchbox houses on a tree-lined street.

I quickly learned that the homes were owned by empty-nester seniors, and the children were bused in from government subsidized apartments. The kids came from all over the globe-- Laos and Vietnam, Tonga and Samoa, Liberia and Nigeria, Mexico and San Salvador. Some even lived in tiny wood-framed houses near a flood plain, bordered by a cement factory, on land their families received as freed slaves after the Civil War. It was what they called low SEC (Socio-Economic) in college. And though we learned how to label student populations, we weren't taught how to effectively reach them. I didn't comprehend this yet. In fact, I was clueless about how much I really didn't know.

In the ten years I taught at Shady Grove, I learned things I didn't want to know--like how to detect a lice infestation and how to recognize the signs of child abuse. I learned things I needed to know--like how to address the learning needs of Emotionally Disturbed students and children who were Attention Deficit.

Learning Disabled, Mentally Retarded, Conduct Disorder, Oppositional Defiant and Autistic all became more than names of disabilities. Instead I saw faces and heard individual stories, as more and more special needs children became fully included in the regular classroom. The students taught me as I struggled to teach them. They were my mentors and this is their story.

The voices will always stay with me and their

stories tell readers much more about public education in America than statistics and test scores.

It's easy to see how the heartbreaking visuals, laced with Jill's compassionate voice and style, bring out the authentic elements, regardless of the sometimes gritty content.

That's what you need to perfect when practicing your unique way of putting words into sentences. Voice and style will sustain the life your writing needs in order for it to breathe authenticity into our imaginations.

STRUCTURE AND FORMAT

POV Pointers

Point of view (POV) is the emotional camera that the reader sees, hears, feels, smells, tastes and moves through when devouring a story. POV can be written in first person or third person, but (please, please, please hear this) if you're a first time novelist, seriously consider writing in third person. It's a preferred POV by most editors who are willing to take a chance on a new author.

Of course immediately you'll think of a half-dozen exceptions. And that's okay. If your story is so strong and fresh that you believe an editor will salivate when reading any line from it, then stick with first person. Most writers, however, have a better chance of marketing their work if it's in third person.

So what are the differences in POV?

First person is written from the "I" perspective, where the main character tells us everything from his or her interpretation of events or sensory details. **Example:** "From the moment I collapsed onto the sofa, I knew my family wouldn't let me rest."

Third person is writing the story from a similar emotional insight, but with the "I" poked out. **Example:** "From the moment Margaret collapsed onto the sofa, she knew her family wouldn't let her rest.

Omniscient or Removed POV means a gamut of things, from telling us every emotional/sensory detail from every character's POV, to bringing us the story in an almost emotionally void presentation. **Example:** From the moment Margaret collapsed onto the sofa, her family wouldn't let her rest.

In each example you can easily see how the content is the same, even though the presentation is varied. The last one tells us what is happening, but doesn't allude to how Margaret feels about the situation. Most readers wouldn't feel as attached to

Margaret if they read the more removed presentation. While there are certainly seasoned writers who do well with this POV, an omniscient downfall can be a lackluster narrative; or worse, it can lead to confusion if a reader can't pinpoint which character to care about early on in a novel.

Mixing POVs

"Whose story is this anyway?" That's usually my first comment if I'm reading a book that jumps from one head to another in an opening chapter. As a reader it makes me dizzy. As a book doctor, it makes me tense to finish reading a client's first three chapters and still have no clue as to who the main character is. Remember: we must be anchored emotionally in one point of view from the get-go.

A common question when I'm giving a workshop on POV is: "Do we have to use only one character's POV for the whole book?" No, the POV doesn't have to come from ONLY one character, but if you switch, you need to follow these solid guidelines:

➢ **Stay in one POV for an entire scene.** That doesn't mean it has to be a chapter length scene, but the text will need to have a specific break before starting another scene. Each scene will have one character's POV that will bring us the current "what's at stake" factor for that character and include a beginning, middle, and end to that scene.

➢ **Give each POV equal time.** In other words, don't throw in a POV from one or two minor characters once or twice in an entire book. The POVs must be presented in a balanced formula.

Example: Study a few of Mary Higgins Clark's novels to see how she changes viewpoint in a balanced, believable manner. She also keeps each character unique by choosing different words and patterns in which each character speaks and thinks.

Another writer who uses differing POVs well is Denise Vitola. Denise is the well-published author of the Ty Merrick Science Fiction mystery series. Her books feature Ty's spitfire, no-nonsense first person point of view, which makes the writing fast-paced, full of sensory detail and vivid in mood. Often, however, Denise will open the books with a third person POV to show events the reader needs to see before Ty comes onto the scene.

And that's one drawback of using only first person. If your main character isn't there to see, hear, feel, smell, or taste something, then the reader can't know about it. Having said that, I have to say there are a whole slew of cozy mysteries with a first person

POV that have sold quite well for decades.

Also, the "I, I, I" factor is often a major structure problem when writing in first person. Starting too many sentences with "I" can make your prose tedious, so I always encourage my clients to try using other ways to start their sentences. Here's an example of too many "I" sentence starters:

I'm Blam Masters, the most dreaded outlaw west of Laredo. I shoot better, drink harder, and spit farther than any man alive. I'll share my lead with anyone who says it ain't so. I've lived nigh on 30 years this way and I reckon to keep right on drinkin' and shootin' till the day I die. . .or at least till I see Rosie again.

Maybe the content is fresh and the voice might be authentic, but those repetitive sentence patterns kill the umph and momentum. Now here's a slight revision that varies the sentence structure while still trying to retain the meat of the first example:

Blam Masters here, the most dreaded outlaw west of Laredo. Everyone says I shoot better, drink harder and spit farther than any man alive. Those that say it ain't so can meet me and my

lead any time, anyplace, just like I've been doing nigh on thirty years. Reckon I'll keep right on this way, drinkin' and shootin' till the day I die. . .or at least till I see Rosie again.

Even though the content is basically the same gruff voice, the presentation has a little more "music" to it. I chose this gruff example so you could feel the rhythm in each, comparing the basics in the first with the smoother structure in the second.

We'll see Blam again later on, but first let's move on to another thing to consider when choosing POV.

Emotion is Motion in POV

Authors who write in first person POV rarely have trouble inserting an emotional undercurrent because everything relates to the "I" perspective. If, however, you're writing in a third person or omniscient POV and you've been told that your prose lacks emotion, you'll need to cure that flat line.

As I mentioned earlier, you must have emotion for the reader to connect and care about your character. One way to do that is to write for a few paragraphs in first person POV. I don't mean to LEAVE those graphs in first person, but do it for a while to fall into the habit of inserting the emotion. I bet you'll find that you can't help but color those sentences with emotional hues. After you've done that, then go back to remove the first person structure and replace it with third person. Here are the Margaret examples again to show how to do it:

FIRST PERSON POV: "From the moment I collapsed onto the sofa, I knew my family wouldn't let me rest."

THIRD PERSON POV: "From the moment Margaret collapsed onto the sofa, she knew her family wouldn't let her rest.

If you need more practice here's a fun exercise I borrowed from Dennis Beck, a friend and writing instructor at Texas Christian University in Fort Worth. I use this exercise a lot in workshops, mostly because it makes writers smile and it really challenges us to use more emotion:

Exercise: Rewrite the story of Jack and Jill in first person POV from Jack's POV as a teenager, with him smitten with Jill. Then do it from Jill's POV in first person. After you finish, take the first person nouns and pronouns out and replace with third person nouns and pronouns.

By practicing this technique a bit, you'll find

yourself inserting emotion without even realizing it. And that's the secret of believable sounding point of view. Also, playing with another POV will help you during those times when you might need to use another POV in your novel—say, maybe during a prologue.

Prologues

Ah, yes, there is much discussion, much debate, and occasionally a fistfight or two about whether or not to use prologues at all. The truth is prologues are not to be thought of lightly, to be tossed in because you simply feel like having one. If you believe your novel must have one, remember that a prologue should be short—no more than five pages if possible, or you'll hamper your chances of selling in today's fiction marketplace.

Prologues need to be used ONLY if their content is vital to the book's main character or plot line and we can't get that info from the main character in the present time frame.

Please read that one more time.

You might use a prologue to give us the POV from a character relaying an experience that occurred years earlier, but is pertinent to the current setting.

Or, you can use a prologue as Denise Vitola does, to give us info we need from a different person than the main character.

Another way to write a prologue is in the form of newspaper clipping, an obituary, or a letter. These types of prologues provide clues or details readers need that for some reason can't yet be seen through the main character's POV.

So yes, prologues are acceptable under certain criteria. If you stick to these suggestions, you'll save yourself potential rejection if you had planned on a lengthy prologue to give back-story. And speaking of back-story . . . .

Flashbacks

Reread the above about prologues and apply the reasoning to flashbacks as well. One major difference and a common problem I see over and over again in my clients' work is that they believe flashbacks are necessary to show us every detail from a character's past.

Please don't do that to your reader. We don't NEED every detail. We only need, and more importantly, we only want the significant info about your characters.

It's perfectly okay--and much more preferred--to discover those necessary bits of insight from a conversation your character is having in the present time frame.

For example: Let's say it's imperative to your book that we readers know that the masked murderer had to have been a fast runner. All witnesses said he killed the chef then disappeared from the restaurant before anyone could catch him. Well, if you have that person bragging earlier in the story about his Blue Ribbons for wind sprints during his college years, then you've given us a clue using a flashback that details the actual track meet.

You've established the believability factor and played fair with the reader. Plus, the bonus is that you gave us that info in a fun-to-learn manner, rather than simply dry narrative. Dry narrative starts to smell like compost—perhaps that's why it's sometimes referred to as narrative dumps.

Narrative Dumps

Dumps of narrative (too much exposition) tend to grow into unsightly heaps of words that daunt our eyesight. Interspersing relevant info into conversations can save the reader from enduring these long passages. And "enduring" is the nicest term I can think of at the moment.

When writers feel compelled to give paragraph-after-paragraph of detailed thoughts, visuals, and movements without ever breaking up those passages with dialogue, we risk encouraging our readers toward snoozing. Which would you rather see as a reader: pages of unbroken prose, or a lot of dialogue? Exactly. So make sure to vary your narrative passages with plenty of conversations that can sneak those bits of character and plot points into your novel without boring your reader.

Everything boils down to quality presentation, regardless of which POV you choose. Follow these foundational principles, and play with each one until you find the best fit for your particular story.

DIALOGUE NECESSITIES:

Dialogue is the life breath of your fiction.

It allows us to hear how each character speaks, using word choices and patterns unique to that character. That balance along with the narrative is what gives an authentic feel to your story. No doubt you understand now why I emphasized using conversations in the above sections. Dialogue is empowering. It invigorates pace and character. It's alive.

You can kill it quite easily, however, if you disregard the dialogue essentials that are outlined below.

Making the Most of Tag-Lines

Tag lines are much more than the famed "he said/she said" speaker identifiers. Yes, tag lines tell us who's speaking, but that's not all they have to be. When distinguishing which character is saying which line of dialogue, remember that if you choose boring tag lines, you'll be rewarded with a bored reader. And if that reader is an editor or agent, you'll be rewarded with a rejection. So think hard when reviewing your dialogue.

Maybe you can hint at emotional insight and setting details through the use of body language. To illustrate, here's another example borrowed from Dennis Beck and his TCU Writing Workshops.

EXAMPLE OF DRY TAG LINES:
   "Good morning, Susan," she said.
   "Hi, Jane," she answered.
   "Want a cup of coffee?" Jane asked.
   "Okay," Susan said.
   "Black?" Jane asked.
   "A little cream," she said.

After reading this dull, but grammatically correct bit of dialogue, do you know anything about these characters? Does either of them sound unique in her speaking voice or pattern? Can we glean anything about their emotional perspectives, or have any idea

where they're about to drink coffee? A café?
A bookstore?

 This is dry dialogue with dry tag lines.

 To liven up your dialogue, vary the dialogue
sections with active tag lines. By active, I mean, use
some movement. Use some gestures, some facial
reactions, some body language.

 Many moons ago a client sent me one of his
first manuscripts, in which his narrative was fresh and
well paced. I thought, yes, this guy is good. Then
when I turned the first page and read his dialogue,
I knew we had major work to do. He would have a
line similar to: **The captain replied, "Blah, blah,
blah…"** for about a page. No kidding. No breaks,
no movement, just "blah, blah, blah." After the closed
quote he'd have another line: **To this the lieutenant
stated, "Yes, sir, blah, blah, blah…"** again straight
dialogue for another page. Talk about monotone.

 Believe me, there was NO feeling of authenticity
for either character in that type of "conversation."

 A short time later, after much practice and
much dedication to learning all elements of fiction
writing, he's well published and is editor of an online
writer's newsletter.

 Writing strong dialogue takes practice. I mentioned this man's story for two reasons: first, to give
you hope that you can write authentic dialogue; and
two, because I wanted you to ponder a few ways to
rewrite the above section using more active tag lines.

Look at the revised version below and remember: active tag lines are either emotional bits of introspective, or motions and facial reactions that SHOW characterand plot insight, as well as setting details.

REVISED EXAMPLE:

"Good morning, Susan." Jane turned from the sink and dried her hands on her apron as her friend sagged into a chair at the kitchen table.

"Hi. . ."

Jane lifted the coffee pot off the gas burner and examined her friend's face. "Want a cup of coffee?"

"Okay," she sighed, absently twisting the engagement ring around her finger.

"Black?"

"A little cream." Susan squeezed her eyes shut, trying to hold back the tears.

Well, now, that's a different chitchat altogether, isn't it? And don't you just love that "sagged" verb? This little revision shows how you can flavor a scene by using meatier tag lines strategically placed within your dialogue.

Now it's your turn to practice, practice, practice. Pick a different setting, with two very different people, and with different tag lines. Will the mood be dark? Angry? Funny? What about if you changed the characters to men? How would that impact which tag lines you choose?

The more you practice inserting tag lines that compliment the dialogue, the more your characters will stand on their own in authentic roles.

USING DIALECT

"Yes, sure, of course," I tell writers all the time they should definitely use dialect when appropriate. Use it sparingly, though, and with a few words that are distinctive with that character's speech. Think of Mary Poppins. Oh, please, it won't kill you.

The way Mary spoke in her English accent was quite different than the way the maids spoke, or the way Bert the Chimney Sweep spoke. Although both were English, Mary was more refined than Bert and her word choices illustrated that. Henry Higgins and Eliza Doolittle are other good examples.

To give dialect further thought, try listing at least five words a character of these backgrounds would commonly use in their spoken verbiage:

A Southern gentleman
A robotic android
A person from Australia
A woman from Ireland
A cultured Opera star
A gangster from the 30s/a modern gang member
A modern day African American businessperson

True, Mark Twain over-used dialect, but it was acceptable for his literary time period. Today it is not. Not for commercial fiction writing, anyway. So when you need to add a certain vocabulary or unique punctuation to show a particular dialect, do so with the "less is more" philosophy to guide you.

A perfect example of the less-works-best philosophy appeared when one of my clients had a female character with a soft, genteel South Carolina lilt. The ONLY time we "heard" the lilt, however, was when the woman spoke a word, such as "wonder," adding an elongated "uh" sound to the pronunciation.

The writer accomplished this by wisely spelling those words differently, as in "wonduh." The odd spellings were infrequent, but interspersed just enough throughout the work to help us hear that lilt each time the woman spoke. If you make your dialect as unobtrusive, it will make a major impact.

Internal Dialogue/Direct Internal Thought

NOW HEAR THIS! Internal Dialogue and Direct Internal Thought is the same thing. Each phrase defines the short, emotional thoughts or mental outbursts that characters "say" in their heads. They aren't enclosed in quotation marks; but they are written in italics.

As in:

Kaye-Lynn's lashes beat double time as Josh unfolded himself from the stretch limo. *Whoa, handsome!*

Or,

Sam jumped back from the opened basement door. His nose wrinkled. *Geez, what a stench!* He slammed the door and waved away the lingering air in front of him.

Some writers confuse all of their characters' thinking times with direct thoughts/internal dialogue. Let me try to clear this up: Obviously we're in the character's head when the narrative turns introspective, but we only "hear" their internal thoughts when it's a short emotional reaction. Here are two examples of characters who obviously are thinking a certain way, but not using **direct thoughts/internal dialogue**:

Kaye-Lynn's lashes beat double time as Josh unfolded himself from the stretch limo. She couldn't believe how handsome he looked. (Notice the last line is a thought in her head, but not a direct emotional outburst.)

Or,

Sam jumped back from the just opened basement door. His nose wrinkled. Geez, what a stench, he thought, and quickly slammed the door shut. (Again, the last line is a thought, but it's accompanied by explanatory text.)

In the first sample, the word "thought" isn't used, rather it's implied; however, it's still not a direct thought, as if it were spoken out loud inside the head. The second blatantly uses the "thought" word, to show it's an introspective thought, but again, it's not a direct thought because the intense emotional outburst isn't there.

Here's a revision of the same examples with the last line italicized to show the direct thought/internal dialogue:

Sam jumped back from the just opened basement door. His nose wrinkled. *Geez, what a stench*! He quickly slammed the door shut.

And as with dialect, using too much **direct thought/internal dialogue** muddies the impact of this technique. It's a tool to swing when a strong emotional point is needed. Only you can decide when it's best for your work, but do take note that dialect and internal dialogue are like salt and pepper: a little seasons a meal, a lot spoils the whole dinner.

Of course I have more to mention about tidying up your prose once you've mastered these basics, as well as tips about marketing and seeking additional editing help. You'll find those in the final sections of this book. So if you're not a non-fiction writer, too, you can fast-forward to Part V now.

Part IV

Doctoring Non-Fiction: A Holistic Approach

CONTENT AND FLOW

Although you stick to facts when writing non-fiction, if you want your work to be as healthy as possible it must also boast two elements used in fiction writing.

First, you should incorporate sensory details for a well-layered narrative. And of course, well-layered is another way of saying marketable. Second, you must add a varied texture in your approach so your writing is also palatable. With those two elements in mind (sensory details and approach) let's tackle the basics of how to examine, probe and heal any maladies in your non-fiction.

Organization of Data and Details

One chronic, but treatable, condition I see in many non-fiction works is a disorganized collection of material. Another problem is a story with too much material. I've been guilty of both in my first drafts, mostly because I'm excited about all I've learned while researching and I want to share every detailed factoid about the subject. It's a fault that could be as messy and as overloaded as one of Dagwood's sandwiches.

Do you remember the word "theme," we were required to define in our Literature classes? At the risk of turning into a bun-topped, fussy school marm, I'd like you to memorize this:

Theme is the pulse of your non-fiction.

Whether developing a feature article, a personal essay featuring witty anecdotes, or a full-length book, you will do yourself a major marketing favor by giving your theme some serious brain time.

Why is theme so crucial?

Because choosing the best theme for each slant will increase your acceptances and your pocket change--you might even make some folding money!

(And yes, you guessed correctly, selling your work is the underlying theme in this book. The over-lying theme, of course, is making your writing the healthiest it can possibly be.)

Consider for a moment an average mailbox full of junk circulars and advertisements, and a few newsletters from various organizations. The one from the *American Disabilities Association* (ADA) will feature articles about the latest advances in the world of disabilities, from pain relief medications to walkers and wheelchairs. It will list web sites, contact info, and support groups of interest to the subscribers. The newsletter's theme is "sharing beneficial information."

Look through that pile of mail again. There's an envelope full of anecdotes about children being helped through your donation to the Happy Hill Children's Home. That newsletter has a completely different slant. They persuade by sharing thank you letters from the children who have been helped with the donations. This group wants to connect with your emotions so you will support their cause.

Different themes equal different presentations of data and details.

When I wrote the biography of John Grisham for Lucent Books, I chose this theme: **no matter how famous Grisham became as a best selling novelist, he still remained an ordinary guy.**

The trick was taking all the information about him and interspersing the theme so that it didn't stick out like gnarly weeds throughout the book. It needed to be more of a subtle rustling in the entire landscape.

One way to do that is to pay extra attention to your seams and segues. Read them out loud to catch any abrupt transitions.

Seamless Styles to Enhance Content

In non-fiction, the chosen approach should remain consistent. If you've elected a persuasive, perhaps even argumentative tone, you shouldn't insert any flip-flop opinions. You'll need to remain true to the established tone, even when presenting a varying statistic. The opposite is true if writing from a removed, hard news perspective, when the personal, more emotional references shouldn't be included.

STRUCTURE AND FORMAT

Choosing the Most Marketable Angles

When I completed the Grisham research, I knew I'd reuse that core research for other projects. After all, if I didn't do that, I'd never make a profit at this writing game.

For example, following the book sale, I wrote an article for the Fellowship of Christian Athlete's Magazine *Victory!*, which included Grisham's strong inner Christian persona mixed with his love of baseball.

A small men's devotional publisher saw that

article and offered to buy an excerpt for their publication. Months later, I sold another article to the American Bar Association magazine, *Student Lawyer* that emphasized Grisham's early college days and his decision to enter law.

And just to illustrate the financial scope, let me be blunt about how much money that research for the only authorized biography of John Grisham has actually netted for its author:

Advance	$1000.00
Balance for completed ms	$1500.00
Total	$2500.00

Now add in the other sales:

VICTORY!	$350.00
Devotional Magazine	$25.00
Student Lawyer	$750.00
Total	$1125.00

Deduct about **$500.00** in expenses it took me to travel to Mississippi where I gleaned hard-to-find info about Grisham's early career from the Mississippi State University John Grisham Library.

You can see that earning as much money as possible from one set of research is essential to filling your writing pockets with more than just bylines.

Parallel Structure

One of the most common trouble spots when writing non-fiction is staying in parallel structure throughout the entire project, whether it's an article or book length manuscript. I suffer the same malady.

Also, remember if you start with a singular structure, keep it singular, same way with plural. I've seen too many inconsistencies within sentences that mangle a perfectly good content. Here's an example:

A writer should never mix their tenses.

(**One revision**: A writer should never mix his or her tense. **A less stilted sounding revision would be**: Writers should never mix their tenses.)

As in the above sample, a sentence can be revised a number of ways to eliminate the problems, but always stay true to your voice and style when rewriting. Otherwise you lose your authentic sound and that reduces the edge that your writing has over somebody else's.

Bulleting and Expanding

Sometimes when we tackle non-fiction, the hardest thing is choosing what to put in and what to leave out. The next hardest thing is choosing how to distribute the research and quotes, and in what manner to layer in that information.

You may have noticed in your own reading that how-to manuscripts lend themselves to the bullet approach:

- It helps narrow focus
- It helps create flow
- It helps organize

Many editors who buy diet plans or self-improvement articles, or craft building stories, prefer this bullet type of approach for those pieces. Reexamine the research you've collected for your topic to determine if this approach is good for your needs.

And of course, once you've chosen which sub-topics deserve the bullets, then it's much easier to choose what parts of your research you'll use when expanding on those topics—maybe by inserting a good source quote or an illustrative anecdote.

Using this approach in query letter writing is also a plus, and it's something we'll discuss more in the Marketing Advice section.

Punctuation and Direct Quotes

I've yet to meet many people who actually enjoy studying punctuation and grammar issues.

"How boring. I want to create!" we say.

Me, too, so hold tight for a miniscule few seconds

and then we'll both get on to more interesting areas of writing.

In the above quotation, note that the **punctuation significant to the statement goes inside the quote marks**—both the period and the exclamation point. And even though the quote is comprised of two complete sentences, the tag line (we say) is not capitalized as a new sentence. It has its own period punctuation.

One question I hear a lot in conference workshops is, "Do we have to use the exact words that someone said if we quote them?" Yes, you should use the exact words as close as you can to the original quote. There are certain margins, however, when you can use your best judgment to tighten the verbiage if your subject has a tendency to overuse a certain word or phrase. Some of these words you'll recognize right away:

You know . . . uhm . . . uh . . . nevertheless . . . and uh.

Some people say the same thing in two or three different ways. Your writing will be tighter, and the quoted person will appear smarter, if you choose the most appropriate phrase from the redundant info. Give us the one that offers the best statistic, the best visual, or the best emotional point of view regarding your topic.

Remember: ANYTHING redundant is worthy of a red ink slash!

We'll cover more about redundant or repetitive phrases in the next section.

Part V

Pumping Up The Heart Rate In All Writing

Identifying Pace Draggers

Of course we want our words to infatuate our readers so much that they'd rather read what we've written than play Free Cell or Candy Crush. That's a mighty big order.

One way to encourage eager page turning is by pumping up the heart rate. To do this we must eliminate passive verbs, unnecessary prepositional phrases, redundancies, wordiness, and repetitive words and phrases.

Passive Phrases

If you can avoid a passive verb or phrase, do

it. Yes, the major, hot-selling authors can use all the WAS verbs they want, but as new authors we must be more inventive. If not, we'll languish in rejection.

So, grab a red pen and circle every one of these words and their varied forms:

was, is, had, be, been, seem, were, appear, become, looked, are.

Now take a second look at the sentences with circled words and see if you can restructure the sentence using a stronger verb. Your first revision might simply be to take the verb out of its passive form and into a more active form. That's a good start. But then you might try to find a more fitting descriptive word instead. For example, which of the following gives a more specific feel to the content?

Sam was walking toward the door.
Sam walked toward the door.
Sam hobbled toward the door.

Passive phrases can be revised with a little time and inventiveness. Again, which example gives a richer feel to the content?

Blam Masters appeared to be getting mad.
Blam Masters' face burned redder than the Arizona desert.

Both sentences let us know that Blam is not a happy gunfighter, but the second sets mood as well as offers a visual.

Some writers ask if every passive verb or phrase should be replaced. Certainly not, or else your writing will be so animated it might lose its authenticity. But the more active voice you offer your reader, the more you keep that reader turning pages.

Prepositional Phrases

Another curse to rich writing is a tool many young writers believe they have to use to achieve rich writing. To be truthful, prepositional phrases are not the end-all of superb writing. Sometimes they're its downfall.

Example: If we overuse prepositional phrases we create such a wordy web that even the most ardent word lover will run and hide from them.

Here's the same sample written with passive and prepositional phrases: If we were to overuse prepositional phrases we would create such a web of wordiness that even the most ardent lover of words would run away and try to hide from them.

Not hard to see the difference, huh? So check

the number of phrases you're relying on and trim, trim, trim.

Redundancies and Wordiness

A first cousin to passive pace killers is redundancy, which leads to wordiness. A quick example:

> **Kaye-Lynn marveled at his strong, muscular arms.**

Well, if they're strong, they're muscular. And if they're muscular, they're strong. Choose one descriptive or the other, and please choose the most visual one. An even stronger revision might be:

> **Kaye-Lynn marveled at the biceps escaping from his short-sleeved t-shirt.**

Each type of revision will hinge on the character's value given to a certain description. Whatever the case, kill any redundant factors where the same info or image comes across in two different ways.

A more subtle redundancy problem comes into play when a bit of information is given in the narrative or tag-lines that is also obvious in dialogue. Let the dialogue stand alone—it's much stronger.

Example:

**John knew he had to tell Mary he loved her.
"I love you," John said.**

(The narrative is redundant of the dialogue.)

REVISION:

John touched Mary's cheek. "I love you."

(Whenever you can imply more emotion, do it!)

Repetitive Words and Structure

We writers have favorite words we use too often. We have favorite sentences. We have habits when forming sentences. We need help.

True, there are effective uses of repetition (I tried one with the "We" sentence starters in the above paragraph). And they're acceptable when you're working toward a specific goal—for a specific emphasis. Most often, however, we need to eliminate needless repetition that creeps into our sentences due to habit or laziness in searching out a fresh description. These problems can deaden our writing. Check for any sentences that begin with too many **The's, As's, There's, or A's.**

EXAMPLE: The youngster picked up the plastic bucket and dumped out its contents. The sand covered his feet and he laughed. The water sloshed over his toes and he wiggled them.

You can feel your interest dying, right? So vary the beginnings. And vary the length, if you want to keep the text energized.

EXERCISE:

Rewrite the previous example in a way that doesn't repeat sentence structure or length.

Now apply those new skills to your own writing until you've trimmed all pace-draggers. Before you know it, your baby will be ready to market.

Nips & Tucks For Success: Marketing Advice

Query Letters

A query letter is the first step in marketing any form of writing. Some editors prefer only hard copy queries through the postal system. Some prefer E-mail queries. Some don't care. Check each publication's guidelines before sending your query so you start off on the right foot with your potential buyer.

Query letters should be **BRIEF** and **BASIC** and include:

* Date
* Publisher name/address
* Greeting
* A hook about your work's content (maybe a statistic

for a non-fiction piece or a point of conflict for a novel)
* Give other pertinent info about the article or book, such as word count and genre
* List any publishing credentials (and yes, contest wins count)
* Mention any clip/SASE enclosures/E-mail attach-ments
* Thanks and Sign off

Try to keep your letters to one, single-spaced page and use Times Roman or Courier, 12-point font. Queries are about the only thing you ever single-space in most commercial markets. Here's a sample of one of mine that helped sell a couple of articles and a workshop. (And although it covers two pages here, it was only one page when typed on a regular 8 ½ x 11 inch letterhead):

July 4, 2001
Christian Kirkpatrick
ENTERPRISE OPERATIONS MANAGEMENT
535 Fifth Avenue
New York, NY 10017
Hello Mr. Kirkpatrick—

As a veteran office manager for several architects, a theater manager, and the leader of various non-profit groups, I know about stress. Who doesn't?

Folks who've attended my "Don't Stress Out, Write It Out!" workshops have learned how to ease their employees and themselves around boulders that stress can cause. I'd like to share these tangible writing insights with your readers.

The 3500 word feature, "4 Ways Writing Can De-Stress Your Workplace," would brim with anecdotes and contain these topics/exercises:

➢ Writing out responsibilities: helps each team member know he is a valued member who is also held accountable to the whole;

➢ Writing out what you want: points out that even as a whole, the team is made up of individuals who need their desires validated;

➢ Writing out what is good: encourages each member to reflect on the positives instead of focusing only on who organized the last Christmas party;

➢ Writing away the anger: allows the necessary frustrations to emerge without causing harm to any other member.

These tips and highlights are based in part on my book from Walking Stick Press, titled, *What Really Matters to Me: A Guided Journal.* I'd love the opportunity to work with you and would welcome an assignment.

A SASE is enclosed for your convenience as well as a bio listing my other writing and editing credentials. Thanks so much for your time and consideration.

--Robyn Conley

You can see where I used parts of my background to connect with the editor and the audience. Then I used bullets to emphasize the topic categories of the proposed article.

Keep in mind that I used this letter in its bare format for queries I sent to other magazine markets by changing the opening background and listing new specifics in the bullets. For example, when I sent it to Christian magazines I used my background as a former church secretary, youth director, and Evangelism chairperson. Then I addressed specifics that involve stress in a church worker's life.

More than anything, a query letter needs to SHOW your writing style, as well as give an editor all the details needed to request the full project.

Sometimes editors prefer you send along a synopsis or overview with your query letters. If so, make sure you follow these tips for each to enhance your chances of selling.

Synopsis and Book Overview Tips

Writing a novel synopsis (the short summary of any fiction book length work), or a book overview (the short summary of a non-fiction book length work) takes some fresh thinking. There are certain basics, but what you need to know first is that you should always use your own voice and style when constructing these selling tools.

Synopsis help first--

One woman came to me at a conference, totally distraught that her novel had yet to be requested after sending out her query with a synopsis. I read the first few pages of her book and the story had a great hook, a lively voice and it made me want to keep reading. Then I looked at her synopsis. Yipes, it read like the book summaries we used to give in middle school. There was no emotion, no voice, just a list of events and characters.

So, when creating your synopsis, remember your style. Remember you're trying to convey a mood and an authentic character. Think of the rapid-fire highlights we see in those movie trailers before the feature presentation comes on the screen. Sometimes you feel as if you've seen a mini-version of the full movie. Make your synopsis that engaging, with those main plot and character points as the focus.

Here are the general rules for writing a winning synopsis that will reward you with the most chances of an editor requesting your entire book:

1) Most often written in **present** tense

2) Range from 2-10 pages, **double-spaced, Courier 12pt**

3) Give the basics (**who what when where why how**)

4) Use your own **STYLE**

5) Use dialogue if appropriate

6) Each synopsis needs a **beginning, middle, and end** (NEVER leave editors hanging by saying they'll have to request the whole thing to see how you wrap up the novel.)

Some of my clients have used a checklist to help them remember all the necessary elements. Here's a copy of the one I give out during my synopsis workshops and to my individual clients.

SYNOPSIS CHECKLIST:

WHO:
WHAT:
WHY:
WHEN:
WHERE:
HOW:

On the next two pages you'll find a sample synopsis of my novel that earned me a manuscript request and eventual sale.

SYNOPSIS SAMPLE:(*LIVING THE RAPTURE,*
Robyn Conley, Hard Shell Press 2000)

Travis Fuller stares at the lifeless body on the gurney. His body. He doesn't panic, doesn't worry about the light surrounding him or the darkness slowly invading its brilliance. Fact is, maybe dying wouldn't be such a bad idea. With his marriage a mess and feeling more like a failure with every passing day, maybe escaping this small West Texas town—even in death—would be the perfect solution.

His thoughts are interrupted when his seven-year-old daughter's spirit passes in front of him. She whispers, "Not yet, Daddy. It's not your turn." Travis' body surges with an electrical current and blood flows again to his limbs. He awakens in the hospital, recovering from a heart attack. His estranged wife, Hayley, is with him, holding his hand, offering an attempt at reconciliation and healing they couldn't find a year ago after their daughter died.

Hayley's easy chatter and genuine soft smile overwhelm him. His heart wants to accept her invitation, yet before he can return home he knows he'll have to tell her about "seeing" Angie. He won't hide his grief any longer. This time they will both have to endure the pain of healing or risk staying apart forever—a tragedy not only for them, but also for their sixteen-year-old son, Dylan.

In spite of lingering fear and doubt, he tells her

about seeing Angie. Hayley's disbelief is immediate. Travis worries she has shut down again. When their friend and doctor walks into the room, Travis recounts all he saw while he was supposedly unconscious. Doc has heard enough about near death experiences to believe him, but Hayley breaks into tears. With an inner strength he hasn't felt in months, Travis knows he has to recover fast to help heal his family.

He may not have earned this second chance at life, but this time he hopes not to fail.

WHAT'S THE STORY? (A pitch line) Some editors and agents say, "Give me your pitch line." This is their way of finding out if you can condense your character and conflict **AND** resolution into one or two concise, engaging sentences. We think synopsis writing is tough—this is murder.

It takes honing in on the core issue with your character and the core circumstances that mold and make the resolution for that character. It also takes a lot of practice.

Here's an example, based on the previous synopsis:

Pitch Line:
Travis Fuller knows he has to recover from his near death experience fast if he ever

hopes to heal his family. He may not have earned this second chance at life, but this time he hopes not to fail.

One way to practice is think of the way you'd describe your book to a friend. That helps condense the main points quick. Then just keep paring that blurb into the most active text you can.

Non-fiction Overviews

Style and voice are equally important for Overviews, which should follow these rules:

1) Written in **present** tense
2) 1-2 pages, **double-spaced, Courier 12pt**
3) **Basics** of book content, **benefit** to reader
4) Use your own **STYLE**
5) Each outline needs a **beginning, middle,** and **end**

Here's a brief checklist for writing an overview:

OVERVIEW:

WHAT—
WHY—
HOW—

Sample Overview: (SPIRITUAL PUSHUPS, Robyn Conley © 1996)

Anyone who isn't blessed with an ideal metabolism knows daily exercise is paramount for physical fitness. Likewise, anyone who isn't blessed with the ability to bounce back from life's blows can benefit from daily doses of joy to pump up their spiritual health.

SPIRITUAL PUSHUPS is a 50,000 word anecdotal guidebook for folks who need gentle reminders to help them choose joy. Taking a cue from the style and content of the popular *Chicken Soup for the Soul* series, this book incorporates both of those positive attractions, yet it goes one step further. It offers an outline about how to write your own recipe for a healthy soul.

Many of the suggestions and tips come from students in the classes I teach about using writing to help heal emotions. The ideas mirror a "physical fitness" routine by including simplistic stretching exercises to loosen up dormant emotional muscles. A constructive mental "pumping up" program is outlined that will offer easy and practical ways to deal with anger, frustration, disappointment, sadness, shame, and even grief.

The format is honest, inspirational, and inclusive to anyone who has ever endured life's hidden bruises. For people uncomfortable admitting emotional pain, these coping suggestions and anecdotes will help validate their feelings and encourage them to tone their inner muscles one manageable set at a time.

YOU PLAY DOCTOR!

Now sharpen your red pens and go through both samples I've listed above. Did I cover the basics? Are any key elements missing? How would you revise a sentence? After you have fun ripping apart the book doctor's writing, then attack your own with the same enthusiasm. Trim and cut, but most important: **SUBMIT!**

Cross Marketing for Greater Sales

Some fiction writers never think of selling to magazines. That's understandable to a degree, but we miss great chances of reusing research and creating new readers if we don't consider the non-fiction market while writing our novels or short stories.

When I spent time at my mechanic's shop, asking endless questions and trying to avoid the oil slicks, I knew I would re-slant some of the things he helped me with for my novel and mold them into a how-to piece about car maintenance.

Together we came up with a top ten checklist that appeared in our local paper. It helped his business and earned me another clip. Diversity is good!

And here's the clincher: when that tiny list appeared, it came with my bio blurb at the end of the article, which listed my website and books. *Voila!* From a simple non-fiction piece, I gained fiction readers. So if you're a fiction author, you might think about broadening your skills to help embrace new readers.

And there's no reason why you non-fiction writers can't revamp your research and possibly market it into a children's magazine or a short story to submit to a contest. Just remember to bring us the info from a child's point of view and use lots of dialogue. Studying the types of sentence structure and word choices for the various ages of juvenile literature is also a necessity.

The point is: try not to limit your career by staying in one box. You're a writer for goodness sakes, so be creative!

Network, Network, Network

Let me be blunt. Not only do you have to be creative, you have to meet editors, agents, and other writers. It's so much easier to make a lasting impression on a potential buyer for your work by meeting that person face-to-face, rather than only through dry queries. With a few exceptions, almost everything I've sold has been related to an in-person meeting. It's essential.

Type in "Writing Conferences" on the search bar and there will be plenty of workshops and seminars to choose from in an area close to you. Save your postage pennies and invest them in a quality conference. The dividends will amaze you. There is companionship of other authors, opportunities to meet the perfect editor or agent, and contests to enter, which will help you learn about submitting.

Eventually, you will land that sale or win that category, and for a writer, there is no better feeling in the world.

Until the next one.

Part VII

Seeking A Second Opinion

BOOK DOCTOR BASICS

Many of my clients are folks with consuming careers. Others are so consumed with writing, that they have no time (or desire) to learn the art of revision. Some are people with great ideas who prefer to have someone else craft those ideas into marketable prose.

I love working as a book doctor with these people nearly as much as I enjoy writing my own stuff. If you feel the need to seek help from an editing professional, you can certainly contact me. Or you can find another book doctor who cares as much about your writing as you do. Having someone care should be a first priority when looking for editing assistance, but there are other concerns as well.

Types of Professionals—

There are many types of editing help available, from simple proofreaders, to tutors, to ghostwriters. Proofreaders usually concentrate only on grammar mechanics and typos; tutors (book doctors) give content editing and critique along with the grammar and typo help; and ghostwriters completely rewrite or start from scratch with interviews and notes from the author.

I've done all three jobs, but many book doctors have specialties regarding genres or types of non-fiction. Others, such as myself, have had success revising just about every type of writing publishable. So, when looking for a professional freelance editor, make sure that person has experience editing your type of work.

Things to Ask the Professional
(Client References, Experience, Credentials)

The fastest way to find the best book doctor for your needs is to ask the tough questions:

- How many published clients does that editor have?
- Will that editor provide a contact list of client references?
- How many years has that editor been working

in the field?

• Is the editor a published author, too?

• What are the fees?

Remember that second opinions are a necessity for making your work the best it can be. If you can't find a critique partner who is a solid objective reader, then you might consider hiring a book doctor. If you do, be sure to ask the above questions so you can avoid any person who might not have hung out an honest shingle.

I want to leave you with the same line I leave all my clients with when I end a critique letter. Please let me know if you have any questions. Any. I'd be happy to discuss your project with you.

You can contact me anytime via E-mail: robconbookdoc@gmail.com or check out my website at www.robynconley.com. I want you to enjoy your writing and watch your bylines grow. You can do it!

About The Author

Robyn Conley, the book doctor, speaks and writes about writing, editing, and marketing what you write. Her latest books include:

THE HEALTHY WRITER'S HANDBOOK- a resource for any writer hoping to have a successful, healthy writing career;

BEYOND THE BRANCHES - Writing and Scrapping Your Complete Family Tree- prompts to help organize and jot down each person's life story;

WHAT REALLY MATTERS TO ME - a journal that helps people discover their goals, and then offers practical tips to make those dreams come true;

INSIGHTS FROM THE JOBSITE – devotions with full-color photos for blue collar workers;

THE COLOR ME BIBLE – a 150 page chronological text overview of the Bible with full-page coloring book pictures;

PRAY THE BIBLE with Paper and Pen - a guidebook to help build intimate conversations with the Lord, for those who might be a bit shy about praying out loud.

Her other published titles include a diversity of topics, such as the biographies: **John Grisham, Cartoonists, Alexander G. Bell**, as well as these juvenile reference books: **Meerkats; Depression; Motion Pictures**; and **The Automobile**.

She has sold to major magazines, such as **The Writer, Writer's Digest, ABA: Student Lawyer**, and many others.

www.ingramcontent.com/pod-product-compliance
Lightning Source LLC
Chambersburg PA
CBHW070433290526
45791CB00005B/1948